I Am the Rain

Written and Illustrated by John Paterson

Dawn Publications

Sometimes I'm the rain cloud

and sometimes I'm the rain.

Sometimes I'm a roadside rapid

roaring down a drain.

I can show you rainbows

in mist or morning dew.

I can be a muddy flood

or a pool of aqua blue.

Once I was a waterfall,
but now I'm just a wave.

At high tide I'm the breaking swell
that daring surfers brave.

In winter I'm the icy flake
that's melting on your nose.

As skiers ski and skaters skate,
I'm sleeping when it snows.

When springtime comes
I melt away and run into a creek.

Waiting, I'm the ocean bay
that searching rivers seek.

Soon the summer sun is back
and warms me with its rays.

I rise in rumbling thunderheads
like castles in the haze.

In fall I sink into a fog
and blanket chilly fields,

with pumpkins touched by morning frost
the harvest season yields.

You'll find me
in the comet high
circling the stars.

I'm also carving canyons deep
on Earth and cousin Mars.

Because of me the land is green.
I'm why the sea is blue.

All of life depends on me.
I'm even part of you.

Soon I'll be a cloud once more,

and then I'll fall as rain.

My circle takes me wide and far,
but I'll come 'round again.

I am water!

My circle is called the Water Cycle.

Condensation:
Water vapor cools as it rises and becomes a cloud of water droplets.

Evaporation:
Water is warmed and becomes water vapor.

Precipitation:
Water droplets stick together until they get so big and heavy that they fall as rain, snow, hail, or sleet.

Collection:
Rain collects in lakes, streams, rivers, and oceans.

EXPLORE MORE — For Teachers and Parents

Note from the Author

Some view water's circular path as a geologic process, while others see it as a metaphor for human experience, and still others as a dynamic force that has shaped life on Earth as we know it today. I wrote this book as a meditation on the ever-changing shape, color, and form of water as it follows its natural cycle. As you read, ask children how each scene fits into water's circular path. Where might water lead them next?

The Science Behind the Poetry

Water is matter and exists in three states: solid, liquid, or gas. Water changes its state depending on the amount of energy (heat) that is available. As the temperature increases, the amount of energy increases, and water molecules move faster.

Solid Water—called *ice, snow, or hail*. When the temperature is at or below freezing, water molecules slow down and are close together in a fixed position. Solid water (like an ice cube) retains its shape as long as it stays cold.

Liquid Water—simply called *water*. When the temperature increases to above freezing, water molecules move around faster, but they still remain close to one another. Liquid water (like a river) flows. It needs a container to hold its shape.

Gas Water—called *water vapor*. When liquid water heats up, the molecules spread out (vaporize) and lose contact with one another. We can't see water vapor. It's invisible.

Why does it rain? Water vapor rises in warm air *(evaporation)*. As it gets higher in the atmosphere, it is cooled and tiny water droplets form *(condensation)*. When the droplets combine with bits of dust, dirt, or pollutants, they form clouds. If the droplets get large enough, they fall as rain *(precipitation)*.

Why does water flow downhill? Gravity pulls water towards the Earth's center of gravity, always following the path of least resistance. The force of gravity prevents water from flowing uphill.

Why do we sometimes see a rainbow? Sunlight looks clear or white to us, but it is actually made of seven colors—red, orange, yellow, green, blue, indigo, and violet. When sunlight shines through water droplets, it bends and these colors are revealed *(refraction)*. When we're standing in the right place, and the angle of the sunlight is just right, we can see a rainbow.

What color is water? Water by itself is colorless. One way it takes on color is from whatever stuff is dissolved in it. For example, dirt particles make the water look brown. Water also gets its color from the way light passes through it. When sunlight shines on clean water, the red, yellow, orange, and green colors are absorbed by water molecules, and we see the remaining colors of blue and purple—the deeper the water, the darker the color blue.

What is a breaking swell? A swell is a long, moving ridge of water. When an ocean swell reaches shallower water, usually along a coastline, it topples over (breaks) and is called a breaking swell.

Are ice and snow really sleeping? No, that's just a poetic way of saying that ice and snow are formed when water molecules slow down. It's comparing ice and snow to people who slow down when they sleep at night.

Do rivers search for the ocean? This is a poetic way of saying that water flows into the ocean. When ice is warmed, it becomes liquid water and immediately begins to follow the path of least resistance, pulled along by gravity. Creeks and streams flow into rivers. Eventually rivers can't go any further and the water forms oceans *(collection)*.

What is a thunderhead? A thunderhead is a type of cloud—*cumulonimbus*. It often produces rainstorms with lightning and thunder. **What causes haze?** Haze forms when very fine particles, such as water droplets, are suspended in the air.

What is fog? Fog is a low cloud that forms near or on the surface of the Earth. **What causes frost?** When air cools overnight, water droplets are formed *(condensation)*. These droplets create frost when it's below freezing or dew when it's warmer.

Is water only found on Earth? Water is found throughout the known Universe. Comets are made of ice, dust, and gas. Scientists have discovered frozen water on Mars, and canyons on its surface tell of a time when large amounts of liquid water carved deeply into the ground.

Why does all life depend on water? Two-thirds of Earth's surface is covered in water. Green plants on Earth are the basis of most food chains, and all green plants need water to live. And animals and people need green plants to live. Our bodies are 80% water!

How does water move in a circle? Water's circle is called the Water Cycle—water forms clouds, falls as rain and snow, moves across the Earth as rivers and glaciers, and flows into the ocean, where it starts its journey again.

Observations and Investigations

A puddle is a good starting point to help children understand water's different forms. Water in a puddle is liquid. When the sun dries up the puddle, the water becomes *water vapo*r—a gas. If it gets cold enough for the puddle to freeze, the water becomes *ice*—a solid. Continue experimenting with water by doing the following activities at home or in the classroom.

SCIENCE: *States of Matter in a Baggie*

You can do this activity as a demonstration or as an experiment in small groups. Mix up a batch of colored powdered drink (such as Kool-Aid) and freeze it in ice cube trays. Ask students what state the water is in and how they know. (It's a solid because it keeps its shape.) Put the ice cubes into a baggie and use masking tape to attach it to a window that gets direct sunlight for most of the day. Observe the bag every half hour. Ask students what they notice. (The solid cubes are being warmed and becoming liquid water, taking on the shape of the container.) After several hours, or the next day, observe the bag. Notice water droplets that have formed on the sides of the bag. Explain that the liquid water became a gas, but couldn't escape the sealed bag so it condensed to form drops and became liquid water again.

ENGINEERING: *Filtering Water*

Challenge small groups of students to design a filter to make muddy water clean and clear. Each design must have a way to collect at least one cup of water. Provide the class with a variety of supplies, including: large and small plastic bottles, plastic cups, masking tape, rubber bands, scissors, spoons, cheesecloth, cotton balls, paper towels, construction paper, and clean fine sand. Have students test their designs and make adjustments as needed. Test each group's filter by pouring muddy water through it. Compare the water's clarity and discuss the results.

MATH: *How Much Rain?*

It's raining, it's pouring . . . but how much? Measure the amount of rain by having students make a simple rain gauge. Cut off the top of a plastic water bottle. Use a ruler and a felt pen to mark increments of 1/4 inch (.5 cm) from the bottom to the top of the bottle. Place the bottle securely in an open area during a rainy season and record your findings. Students can take turns reading the gauge and recording the daily amount of rain. Create a bar graph to show the amount of rain over time.

Taking Care of Water

The care of rivers isn't a question of rivers, but of the human heart — Tanaka Shozu, highly-esteemed Japanese naturalist

There is a constant amount of water on Earth. The water coming out of your tap was once a cooling drink for a dinosaur. It was once an ocean wave. It may have been frozen in a glacier in Antarctica or flowed in a river through a rainforest. We depend on this finite amount of water, and it's important that we help take care of it.

Why I Love Water

The first step in water conservation is appreciating water. Look back at the illustrations and have children make a list of the activities that people are doing. Then have children add to the list by identifying the ways they interact with water, including playing in it. Ask children to put a heart next to each item on the list that is important to them or that they like to do. Have them draw a picture of one of their items. The picture can become the basis for a poem or story.

Water Saving Tips

Discuss ways children can help save water. You may want to

- use a gallon jug or a liter bottle filled with water as a visual aid when discussing how much water is saved.
- Turn off the tap when you brush your teeth, morning and night. Save up to 8 gallons (30 liters) per day.
- Take a shower rather than a bath. Save up to 60 gallons (227 liters).
- Turn off faucets tightly so they don't drip. Save 34 gallons (129 liters) per year for each faucet.
- When washing your hands, don't let the water run while you lather.
- Instead of running the tap until water gets cold, keep a container of cold water in the refrigerator.

Scan this code to go to free online activities and standards-based lesson plans, including "Cloud in a Jar,' "How to Make a Rainbow,' and "Putting the 'I' in Poetry.' Or go to www.dawnpub.com and click on "Activities' for this and other Dawn books.

More Books About Water from Dawn Publications

Pitter and Patter—Take a wild ride through the water cycle with Pitter and Patter, two drops of rain that journey through different watersheds.

A Drop Around the World—From Maine to Mumbai, a single rain drop touches plant, animal, and human life all around the world.

Over in the Ocean: In a Coral Reef—Explore the animals of the coral reef through this fresh adaptation of the traditional song "Over in the Meadow.'

Over in a River: Flowing Out to the Sea—Rivers are teeming with life! Discover river animals, their "baby' names, and their actions.

On Kiki's Reef—Marvel at the life on a coral reef as you follow the adventures of a sea turtle (Kiki), from a tiny hatchling to a gentle giant.

Salmon Stream—The drama of the salmon's life cycle, told in cumulative verse, carries you from stream to ocean and back again.

A Swim through the Sea—Stunning illustrations take you on an alphabetical tour of the undersea world.

Avery Paterson Photo

As a child, **John Paterson** was fascinated by the changing form, steady purpose, and life-giving magic of water. Later, he chased rivers throughout the country as a white-water kayaker and raft guide. Professionally, he has helped craft stories of nature and culture for museums and other educational organizations including the Field Museum and the Garfield Park Conservatory in Chicago. He lives with his wife and two children in Northbrook, Illinois.

"This grand show is eternal. It is always sunrise somewhere; the dew is never all dried at once; a shower is forever falling; vapor is ever rising. Eternal sunrise, eternal sunset, eternal dawn and gloaming, on sea and continents and islands, each in its turn, as the round earth rolls." — John Muir

For Amy, Graham and Avery — *JP*

Published by Dawn Publications, an imprint of Sourcebooks eXplore
P.O. Box 4410, Naperville, Illinois 60567-4410
(630) 961-3900
sourcebookskids.com

Library of Congress Cataloging-in-Publication Data
Names: Paterson, John, 1958- author, illustrator.
Title: I am the rain / written and illustrated by John Paterson.
Description: Nevada City, CA : Dawn Publications, [2018]
Identifiers: LCCN 2017018746 | ISBN 9781584696155 (hardcover) | ISBN 9781584696162 (pbk.)
Subjects: LCSH: Water--Juvenile literature. | Hydrologic cycle--Juvenile literature.
Classification: LCC GB662.3 .P39 2018 | DDC 553.7--dc23 LC record available at https://lccn.loc.gov/2017018746

Special thanks to editor and rainmaker Carol Manor, without whom this book would not have seen the light of day! —JP

Book design and computer production by
Patty Arnold, *Menagerie Design & Publishing*

Source of Production: Wing King Tong Paper Products Co. Ltd.,
Shenzhen, Guangdong Province, China
Date of Production: April 2022
Run Number: 5026204

Printed and bound in China.
WKT 10 9 8 7 6 5 4 3 2